The Pre-Marriage Course Leader's Guide, Revised and Updated
© 2003, 2020 by Alpha International

Published in Nashville, Tennessee, by W Publishing Group, an imprint of Thomas Nelson. W Publishing Group and Thomas Nelson are registered trademarks of HarperCollins Christian Publishing, Inc.

ISBN 9780310122487

First Printing 2020 / Printed in the United States of America

The Pre-Marriage Course
Leaders' Guide

Contents

Welcome

Many years ago a government minister said to us, "We know that a strong society is built on strong families, and strong families are built on strong marriages. That's why we're interested in these Marriage Courses."

We are so glad that you have decided to run The Pre-Marriage Course—to invest in relationships in your community and, in turn, invest in your own relationship. We hope you find the experience as enjoyable and rewarding as we do.

This Leaders' Guide is designed as a quick-reference guide to setting up and running your course. We find it helpful to have it with us when we are hosting a session. The checklists and timetables are particularly helpful for keeping us on track.

Please get in touch if you have any questions and do let us know how you get on.

Nicky and Sila

Nicky & Sila Lee
Creators of The Marriage Course

Introduction

The Pre-Marriage Course has been in development at Holy Trinity Brompton (known as HTB), London, since 1985. Since then, The Pre-Marriage Course and The Marriage Course have been run in 127 countries around the world, reaching nearly one million couples.

The Pre-Marriage Course is a series of sessions designed to help couples build strong foundations for their future by equipping them with the tools and practical skills they will need, such as learning to communicate well, appreciating their differences, exploring beliefs and values, embracing commitment, and building a healthy and supportive relationship.

While based on Christian principles, The Pre-Marriage Course is relevant to all couples, whether they have a faith background or not, and we welcome every couple whether they are engaged or just exploring the idea of marriage.

In 2020 The Pre-Marriage Course was updated and remade—with five video episodes hosted by Nicky and Sila Lee, featuring expert insights and drawing on the real experiences of couples from all around the globe. Courses run in a variety of venues and contexts, from churches and community centers to cafés and homes.

Each session of The Pre-Marriage Course starts with something to eat and drink—this helps to create a welcoming, romantic environment—followed by a talk and times for private conversations for each couple. Each guest is given a *Guest Journal*, which provides guidance for each conversation and is an essential part of the course.

For more information, please visit **alphausa.org/marriage** where you'll be able to watch training videos, access our latest resources, and register your course.

05

How to run

The Pre-Marriage Course is easy to run. We have a series of filmed episodes of the course content, which are available to buy and download on our website when you register a course.

Head to **alphausa.org/marriage** to get started—to register your course, to download the episodes, and to access the short training films. And don't forget to buy enough *Study Journals* for guests to have one each (two per couple).

Using the filmed episodes for your talks gives you time to focus on creating a welcoming, hospitable, and relaxed environment for your guests.

There are clear prompts on the video when you need to pause to give couples time for a private conversation. These prompts match the guidance in the *Study Journal*. You'll also find the timings of these conversations for each session in the "Session Guide" section of this guide.

Everything you need to know about how to run the course is at your fingertips at **alphausa.org/marriage**.

Creating the experience

Creating a romantic, relaxed, and intimate atmosphere is an essential part of running The Pre-Marriage Course.

The welcome that couples receive and the atmosphere when they arrive will leave a lasting impression. Some couples may feel daunted and wonder whether they will be asked to share personal details about their relationship with others. Creating the right environment with the feel of an intimate date night will help to reassure them that the discussions they have will only be between the two of them.

This kind of atmosphere helps to create a safe space in which couples are more likely to open up to their partner and have meaningful conversations that are key to the course.

07

Choose the right venue

For a smaller course an ideal venue may be a home—this can be just like hosting friends. In this setting, you might choose to eat together first before sitting as couples for the session's episode.

For a bigger course you will obviously need more space. This could be a church, a community center, or even a local restaurant or café.

Wherever you're hosting your course, you will need to be able to provide three things: something to eat and drink, a screen to watch the talk, and enough space to allow each couple to have their own private conversations.

Decor and lighting

The course should provide a relaxed space where guests feel like they're out on a date. If you have the space, individual tables for two will help provide a feeling of intimacy and privacy. Candles, soft background music, low lighting, and flowers on the tables all help to create the right mood.

It's all about food

Every session starts with something to eat and drink. This helps guests to unwind from their day and is a chance for each couple to refocus on each other ahead of the talk. What you choose to serve will vary depending on where you are in the world, the size of your course, and what time of day you're hosting it.

Serving dessert and tea and coffee when the couples are having their longest conversation helps to give guests the feeling that they've been hosted throughout the session.

If possible, it's a good idea to serve the tea, coffee, and dessert at their tables in order not to detract from the mood you've created.

Suggested room layout

Arrange separate tables for two sufficiently far apart to ensure each couple's conversations are private. Make sure everyone can see the screen. Allocate a space to put coats and bags.

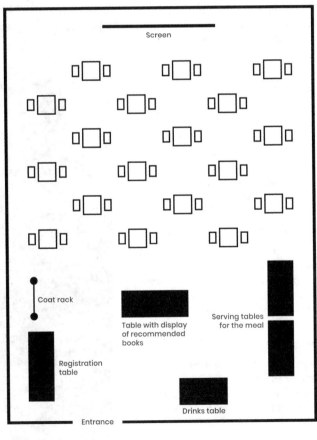

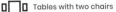 Tables with two chairs

09

Building a team

The Pre-Marriage Course is best run with a team. It's a great opportunity for people in the church to get involved, regardless of their life stage or relationship status. Depending on the size of your course, you will need enough volunteers to fill some, or all, of the following roles.

Course hosts

Course hosts usually open and close the evening and make announcements. They don't need to worry about giving talks as we recommend you use the video episodes to deliver all the course content. These are available on **alphausa.org/marriage** when you register your course.

Administrator

Your administrator will manage registration details, collect payments (if you are charging guests to help cover your costs), and ensure that all the resources you need are available for each session.

Room stylist

This person will use their skills to transform the venue into a special date night experience for the guests where couples feel relaxed and can enjoy an evening together.

Technical team

When this goes well, no one even notices there is an operator; but when it doesn't, everyone notices! The technical team runs the videos, plays background music, and displays any slides.

Caterer

Do you know someone who loves preparing food and may be willing to help with your course? If you're running a larger course, you could arrange for an outside caterer to supply an affordable meal.

Welcomers and additional hosts

Making people feel welcome and relaxed as they arrive is essential. The welcomers will be the first people that guests meet, so try and think of the friendliest people you know and ask them to be part of the team.

For a larger course it's helpful to have additional hosts to help with welcoming, serving drinks, and being available to guests who may seek further support or advice.

Counseling support

Our experience is that a few couples on each course ask for additional support, some of whom need ongoing specialist help. Prepare for this with a referrals handout of local professional counselors.

Set up and tear down team

Depending on the size of your course, you might want to identify people who can help set up the venue for each session and tear it down afterwards.

Prayer team

Prayer is a vital aspect of running The Pre-Marriage Course. You could ask one person, or a team of people, to commit to praying for all the different aspects of your course—from the logistics, to the team and the guests.

11

Promoting your course

Most couples come on The Pre-Marriage Course because of a personal invitation. Telling others about their experience of the course helps to dispel the myth that The Pre-Marriage Course is only for couples who need help. The reality is that it's relevant for any couple wanting to invest in their relationship and think about their future.

The following **six tips** will help to equip your team, members of your church, and couples who've already been on the course to tell others and invite them to your course.

01

Ask couples to tell stories about their experience

Ask them: What did you like and appreciate about the experience? What difference did it make to your relationship?

02

Explain that the course is for any couple exploring marriage

Whatever their situation—whether they are engaged or thinking about marriage, whether or not they are churchgoers, and whether their relationship is in good shape or they are struggling—The Pre-Marriage Course is for them.

03

Paint a picture of what the course looks like

Explain that it's like a date night and reassure couples that they will not be asked to discuss anything about their relationship with anyone but their partner.

04

Give the date, time, and venue

As you approach the end of one course, it's helpful to have invitations for the next course printed and ready for guests to give out to their friends with their personal recommendation.

05

Spread the word

You can access a number of promotional resources online when you register a course. They include stories of relationships deeply impacted by the course as well as flyers, posters, and banners. Visit **alphausa.org/ marriage**.

06

Register your course

Every time you run The Pre-Marriage Course, log in and register the details at **alphausa.org/ marriage** This will enable potential guests in your area to find it on our searchable map.

13

Common mistakes

We've identified the most common mistakes and misconceptions that people have about running The Pre-Marriage Course. We want to pass on what we've learned over the years to help you run the best course possible.

"I have to have a perfect marriage to run a course"

Fear not, there is no perfect marriage! All you need is a desire to help others invest in their relationship. You certainly don't need to be a marriage expert—all the course content is available to download at **alphausa.org/marriage**.

"I need to adapt the course for my context"

The experience of thousands of hosts around the world is that the courses work in many, very different, cultures and contexts. Our encouragement is to keep to the basic course structure, content, and timing—we've found they work together to give couples the right amount of space to process what they are learning and to put it into practice.

Importantly, resist the temptation to add to or take away from the course material, to merge sessions, or extend or cut the conversation times.

"It's a course, so it should look like a classroom"

When the guests walk in, we don't want them to feel that they're attending a class or a lecture, or even a sermon; we want them to feel like they're on a date. A warm welcome and special atmosphere cause people to feel safe and helps them to open up to their partner and have those important, honest, and intimate conversations.

"Perhaps we should also do some group work. . ."

It's easy to think that it would be helpful for people to share what's going on in their relationship and to learn from each other's experiences. But couples come on The Pre-Marriage Course for a variety of reasons, and knowing that the conversations between them are totally private and that there is no group work encourages many couples to attend who otherwise would not consider it.

"It's only for couples in our church"

The Pre-Marriage Course is for any couple, not just those in your church. It's actually a great way for the church to reach out and meet an important need in society. The course gives hope and encouragement, as well as practical tools, for any couple from any background, with or without a Christian faith. After doing The Pre-Marriage Course some couples will be inspired to explore the Christian faith further by trying Alpha.

"We've run it once, so now we're done"

In our experience, the majority of people who come on The Pre-Marriage Course do so because it has been recommended by someone who has found it helpful. The benefit of running multiple courses (two or three times per year, for example) is that it builds momentum and allows those who have completed the course to share their experiences and invite others to attend a future course.

In addition, we invite all the couples on The Pre-Marriage Course to come back to do The Marriage Course two years or so into their marriage. By this time they will be aware of the relevance of all the topics we address. They might then go on to become a support couple for couples on The Pre-Marriage Course. Having these two courses running in parallel on an ongoing basis provides a way of establishing and maintaining healthy marriages.

15

Support couple training

What is a support couple?

A support couple's role is to take an interest in a couple's relationship and to provide a model of what a normal, healthy marriage looks like. The basic requirements for being a support couple are to have been married for two years or more and to have previously completed The Marriage Course.

Support couples don't need to be experts in marriage and certainly don't need to have the perfect marriage (as we've said, no one does!). They simply need to be happy to invite a couple into their home, to offer them hospitality, and to be willing to share from their own experiences of marriage.

The primary task of a support couple is to facilitate an open conversation between the couple, and we provide a tool to help make it easier: the Couple Survey.

What is the Couple Survey?

The Couple Survey is a highly effective tool for supporting couples who are engaged or exploring marriage.

It's an online questionnaire comprised of 150 statements which each person fills in separately and without consulting their partner, ideally before attending the first session of The Pre-Marriage Course. Once they have both completed and submitted their answers, their results are analyzed to produce a report, which is then sent to their assigned support couple in a private link prior to their scheduled meeting.

The Couple Survey isn't a compatibility test, but rather a snapshot of their relationship at a moment in time. The report guides the conversation between the support couple and the guest couple to the issues that are most relevant and important for them to discuss.

Training support couples

To equip support couples effectively for their role in interpreting the Couple Survey Report and discussing its findings with guests, please ensure that they watch our online support couple training videos, which include:

• A guide for how to interpret the Couple Survey Report
• A walk-through example of a Couple Survey meeting
• Guidance on how to handle sensitive issues that may arise

Find the support couple training videos at **alphausa.org/marriage**

17

Session structure

Each session of your course will be about two-and-a-quarter hours long, including the meal. You can find specific timings for each session on pages 21–27. These follow the timings for our course in London, but you can adjust the start time depending on what is most suitable for your guests in your context.

....

Welcome

Some guests are apprehensive on the first evening; a warm welcome will help them relax.

The meal (30 minutes)

This enables you to nurture an atmosphere of a date for the couples and gives them time to connect.

Announcements and recap (up to 10 minutes)

After giving any announcments, we provide couples with the opportunity to go back over what was covered in the previous session(s). Refer to the individual session guides, starting on page 21, for more details.

Episode and conversations (up to an hour and 35 minutes)

The episodes are interspersed with times for private conversation—these are opportunities for them to talk together about an area of their relationship. These conversations each last from five to fifteen minutes. We recommend you play some background music to maintain the feeling of privacy for each couple.

The timing of all the conversations will be indicated within each filmed episode and can also be found in the session guides starting on page 21.

Continuing the conversation

Each session in the Study Journal is followed by a section entitled
"Continuing the conversation". This encourages guests to look at their
calendars and plan a date together in the coming week. There may be
time for them to plan this before they go home at the end of the session.

....

There are questionnaires available for guests to complete at the start
of the final session of The Pre-Marriage Course—these provide helpful
feedback for next time around. You can find them when you register your
course on **alphausa.org/marriage**.

19

Quick checklist

To make sure you're prepared and ready for each session, we've put together a quick checklist of things you'll need to run the course and create a great atmosphere.

. . . .

- ☐ This *Leaders' Guide*
- ☐ The Pre-Marriage Course episodes—purchase the DVDs or download the episodes at **alphausa.org/marriage** and register your course details
- ☐ *Study Journals*—one per person
- ☐ TV screen or projector—to play the episodes
- ☐ Background music—to be played during the meal, while the guests are having their private conversations, and at the end of each session
- ☐ Catering: food and drink at the start and during the session
- ☐ Tables and chairs
- ☐ All the extra things to make the atmosphere special—suitable lighting, tablecloths, flowers and vases, candles, table napkins
- ☐ A list of guests who've registered for the course
- ☐ Pens—for guests to make notes in their journals
- ☐ Spare *Study Journals* to lend out in case any guests forget to bring theirs to a session
- ☐ Microphone—for larger groups
- ☐ Book table or stand—should you want to display any of the recommended reading
- ☐ End-of-course questionnaires for the final session only

21

Session Guide

....

Session 1
Communication

Overview

This session considers how communication is affected by personality, family background, and circumstances. Couples look at what it means to talk about their feelings and practice listening to each other.

Timetable

6:30   Be ready—guests often arrive early!

6:45   Welcome and drinks

6:50   Meal

7:15   5-minute warning

7:20   Welcome

- Relax—you won't be asked to discuss anything about your relationship with anyone but your partner

- If you get stuck at any point on the course, please let us know. We or another couple would be very happy to see you privately. We also have details of a counsellor we could put you in touch with if necessary

....

7:25   Play **Episode 1 | Communication**

7:32   Conversation 1: Different expectations (5 minutes)

7:43   Conversation 2: How we communicate (5 minutes)

7:52   Conversation 3: Family styles of communication (10 minutes)

22

23

Session 2
Conflict

Overview
Conflict can either destroy a relationship or, if handled well, strengthen it. In this session, couples consider how to appreciate their differences, look for solutions together, and heal the ways they hurt each other.

Timetable

6:45	Welcome guests with a drink
6:50	Meal
7:15	5-minute warning
7:22	Recap of Session 1

- Tell each other something new that you learned about marriage on Session 1 and something new you learned about your partner
- Then tell each other what it felt like to be listened to in Conversation 5, "Effective Listening"

....

7:25	Play **Episode 2 | Conflict**
7.:39	Conversation 1: Rhinos and hedgehogs (10 minutes)
7:57	Conversation 2: Recognising your differences (10 minutes)
8:17	Conversation 3: Using the five steps (10 minutes)
8:40	Conversation 4: Healing hurt (15 minutes)

....

8:58	End of session

Session 3
Commitment

Overview
Commitment lies at the heart of the marriage covenant and is reflected in traditional marriage service vows. In this session, couples consider the meaning of these vows and then look at how to live out this commitment in everyday life.

Timetable

6:45 Welcome guests with a drink

6:50 Meal

7:15 5-minute warning

7:20 Recap
- Look back at Session 2 to remind yourself what was covered
- Then discuss with your partner which of your differences cause conflict and how these could be complementary in your relationship

....

7:25 Play **Episode 3 | Commitment**

7:33 Conversation 1: The benefits of marriage (5 minutes)

7:53 Conversation 2: Roles and responsibilities (10 minutes)

8:10 Conversation 3: The marriage vows (10 minutes)

8:25 Conversation 4: Discussing your finances (10 minutes)

8:46 Conversation 5: Parents and in-laws (10 minutes)

....

9:00 End of session

25

Session 4
Connection

Overview
This session explores how love needs to be nurtured in a marriage. Couples do this through building their friendship, discovering how the other feels loved, and developing their sexual relationship.

Timetable

6:45	Welcome guests with a drink
6:50	Meal
7:15	5-minute warning
7:20	Recap

• Ask your partner what they found most helpful for your relationship in Session 3

....

7:25	Play **Episode 4	Connection**
7:37	Conversation 1: Building friendship (10 minutes)
7:56	Conversation 2: Discover your love languages (15 minutes)
8:26	Conversation 3: Talking about sex—Part 1 (10 minutes)
8:43	Conversation 4: Talking about sex—Part 2 (10 minutes)

....

8:56	End of session

Remember to have your end-of-course questionnaires ready to give to guests at the final session next week. These can be found at **alphausa.org/marriage**

Session 5
Adventure

Overview
In this final session, guests have the opportunity to discuss their priorities and goals for the future, the roles they expect to fulfill, and the building of spiritual togetherness.

Checklist
- End-of-course questionnaires, which can be found at **alphausa.org/marriage**
- Invitations to your next Pre-Marriage or Marriage Course

Timetable

6:45   Welcome guests with a drink

6:50   Meal

7:15   5-minute warning

7:20   Announcements and recap

- See if you can remember the order of importance of the love languages for your partner. Look back to Session 4, Conversation 2, if you can't remember

- If you have your next course planned, make invitations available and encourage guests to invite their friends

- Invite guests to complete the end-of-course questionnaire (explain that this will serve as a helpful recap of the whole course for them as well as being helpful to you to improve the experience of guests on future courses)

. . . .

27

7:30	Play **Episode 5 | Adventure**
7:40	Conversation 1: Expressing appreciation (10 minutes)
8:05	Conversation 2: Reflecting on your upbringing (15 minutes)
8:33	Conversation 3: Working out your priorities (10 minutes)
8:50	Conversation 4: Adventurer or nurturer (10 minutes)

....

| 9:05 | End of session | Ask guests to put any final comments on their end-of-course questionnaire and hand it in before they leave. |

To purchase DVDs and study journals for The Marriage Course and The Pre-Marriage Course, visit **churchsource.com/collections/alpha -marriage**, or pay for digital access. For the first time ever, all the talks will be available to purchase online; while access to the updated training videos, introductory videos and downloadable Leaders' Guides will be available at no charge at **alphausa.org/marriage**.

Follow us on social media @marriagecourses

Alpha USA
1635 Emerson Lane
Naperville, IL 60540

800.362.5742

questions@alphausa.org
alphausa.org

@alphausa

Alpha Canada
#101-26 Fourth Street
New Westminister, BC V3L 5M4

800.743.0899

support@alphacanada.org
alphacanada.org

@alphacanada

Alpha in the Caribbean
Holy Trinity Brompton
Brompton Road
London SW7 1JA UK

+44 (0) 845.644.7544

americas@alpha.org
caribbean.alpha.org

@alphacaribbean

Pay It Forward
When more churches run Alpha, more guests meet Jesus. It's that simple.
Alpha comes alongside the Church to train, equip, and provide effective
resources to help them in their mission, all completely free of charge.
We can do this because of your support in time, prayer, and donations.
We are incredibly grateful for your partnership on this journey.

If you would like to help make this possible for more churches and
guests to experience, you can give online at:

USA: alphausa.org/give | Canada: donate.alphacanada.org